May the beauty of the
eagles bring you joy.
Jess & Peggy

LLANO
BALD EAGLE
NEST

A THREE YEAR PICTORIAL HISTORY
OF THREE ADULTS
AND THE EAGLETS THEY RAISED

BY JESS AND PEGGY THOMPSON
Forward by Dale Schmidt, Texas Parks and Wildlife Technician IV

Cover page photo: Two adult bald eagles with two eaglets of the Llano County, Texas nest.

Title Page photo: The three adult bald eagles of the Llano County, Texas nest.

ISBN 1-59152-029-0

Text by Jess and Peggy Thompson

Photographs by Jess and Peggy Thompson

Produced by Sweetgrass Books, A Division of Farcountry Press
P.O. Box 5630, Helena, MT 59604

Created, produced and designed in the United States

Printed in Korea

This book is dedicated to

YOU

YOU, the free and beautiful bald eagle;

YOU, the visitors who came to view the nest and its occupants;

YOU, the ones who followed the photos on our web site;

YOU, the residents, businesses and agencies of Llano and Burnet counties who not only put up with all the tourists on the roadside, but were happy to give them information on how to get there and all the current activity;

PREFACE

The Bald Eagle (Haliaeetus leucocephalus) remains on the state and federal status list of threatened species. However, in Texas and across the nation Bald Eagle numbers continue to increase. In Texas, the number of Bald Eagle nests have increased from 13 active nesting pairs in 1982 to 160 active nesting pairs that raised 240 eaglets in 2005, according to Texas Parks & Wildlife Department surveys.

The Bald Eagles in Llano County, Texas can be divided into 2 groups, wintering and nesting. Wintering Bald Eagles may be seen from December to March. Most wintering or northern Bald Eagles can be seen on the north end of Lake Buchanan, or in remote parts of the county near a river or body of water. Wintering Bald Eagles will leave the Llano County area in March, and return to northern states to breed and raise their young.

Bald Eagles that nest in Texas are nesting or southern Bald Eagles. Nesting Bald Eagles arrive in Llano County as soon as October and will leave the nest site by June. Bald Eagles will use the same nest year after year, usually adding more sticks making the nest larger each year. A new nest site will be constructed if the nest used the previous year is destroyed. A nest may become so large that the weight of the nest might break the limb of the tree and destroy the nest, causing the nesting pair to relocate to a new nest site. Mating occurs in December, the female will lay one to three eggs, most commonly 2 eggs. Both the male and female will incubate the eggs; incubation is 34 to 36 days. 1 to 2 eaglets will usually hatch. Eaglets will grow rapidly and fledge from the nest in 11 to 12 weeks. At the time of fledging, the eaglet will have a wing span of 6 to 7 feet and weigh 10 pounds or more. An eaglet can be identified by its brown feathers with white feathers intermixed on the body and wings. A Bald Eagle will obtain the white head and tail feathers at 4 to 5 years of age. A mature male Bald Eagle will stand up to 3 feet tall and have a wing span of 6 to 7 feet and weigh 7 to 10 pounds. The mature female Bald Eagle will be somewhat larger than the male. Bald Eagles will mate at 4 to 6 years of age and will mate for life. If one of the mates dies, then the remaining Bald Eagle will find a new mate. Bald Eagles can live up to 30 years in the wild.

Historically, a nesting Bald Eagle pair has used the Llano River in eastern Llano County, Texas since the late 1980's. The Llano River provides a source of water, food and suitable trees for nesting. This Bald Eagle pair has had 3 active nest sites along a one half mile stretch of the Llano River. All but the present nest site has been destroyed by natural causes. The current nest site, which was established in 2004, is located 130 yards from a state highway on private property and has been a major tourist attraction for Llano County. Visitation by the public increases when the eaglets are large enough to be seen in the nest which are usually visible by February through the spring until the eaglets leaves the area in late May. Visitors to the nest site may include several hundred during a weekday, to close to a thousand visitors on the weekends. Even though this is a highly visible and visited nest site the adult nesting pair continues to raise eaglets (2 in 2004, 2 in 2005, and 1 in 2006).

Not only does the nesting pair continue to return to the same nest site and tolerate the human observers, a third adult Bald Eagle may also be seen on the nest or perched in a nearby tree. The third adult Bald Eagle is believed to be an older female due to size and appearance. The nesting pair not only tolerates the third adult, but allows it to bring food to the nest, rebuild the nest, and be in the nest with the eaglets. Nesting trios are a rare event, but have been recorded at other nest sites in the United States.

Through protection of habitat, and of the species, the Bald Eagle population will continue to increase and flourish in Texas for future generations of Texans to enjoy.

Dale Schmidt
Wildlife Technician IV
Texas Parks & Wildlife Department

INTRODUCTION

This book is an effort to share with you our observations through three seasons at a bald eagle's nest in Llano County, Texas. It is not a scientific study, though we share a lot of different behaviors we saw at the nest. It is just a few of the hundreds of photos we took and a few of the incidents that occurred. Hopefully, we didn't leave out many of your favorite shots or stories. Although the book is divided into a narrative of the three years we observed the nest, there are also individual pictures from all seasons scattered throughout the book.

The majority of the pictures were taken with Nikon digital cameras and a 600mm lens. The nest in the photos is approximately 135 yards from the side of the road where the photos were taken. No attempt has been made in any way to alter the photos. If there is a stick in the way of a clear shot of an eagle's head, it is because that is how the action occurred. All the shots were made from the same location at the Llano nest and none were posed or staged. The eagles are totally free and wild.

All the photos included in the book are posted on our web page: www.cottonwoodphotography.com. Check it out, there are even more eagle pictures as well as other wildlife and nature shots.

We are grateful to the Texas Parks and Wildlife Technician Dale Schmidt for his comments in the Preface. His preparation of information helped so many at the sight learn more about the bald eagle.

Our thanks also go to the many photographers who came by and from whom we learned so much as we shared ideas and talked about all the equipment needed for wildlife pictures. Second only to the joy of watching the eagles was the joy of meeting so many of you.

A special note of thanks to the Llano National Bank of Llano and Buchanan Dam for going the extra mile in service as they shared news and photos of the nest with so many. The same can be said of the Llano Chamber of Commerce who so graciously answered so many questions about the eagles.

How many special notes of thanks can one have? There has to be at least one more, to the "Texas Hill Country Magazine" for its excellent coverage of the eagles mixed in with all the other fascinating things there are to do in the Texas Hill Country.

We also want to express our gratitude to Richard and Gail Buquoi along with Dale and Seawillow Schmidt for their willingness to help in proofreading the text.

May these photos and comments give you just a glimpse of the awe we felt at watching one of God's most graceful creatures.

FIRST NESTING SEASON

When we first started watching the eagles' nest, we knew few facts about bald eagles but were nonetheless impressed with their beauty and wanted to learn more. Thus began a process of internet research and on site observation. It did not take long to be able to anticipate when they would take off from a perch as they put their talons in just the right position and thrust themselves into the air. The shot to the left was taken on a cold day with sleet falling.

It was the next day when snow actually fell at the nest area. Although it did not last very long, it made for a beautiful sight on the nest and limbs as an adult eagle brought in a fish to feed the young eaglets. Since this nest is located on the banks of the Llano River the eagles did not have to go far to find their preferred food, fish.

With a little study, we discovered that this nest, with three adult bald eagles all working together, or cooperating, was very unusual. Since the coloration of the male and female adult eagle is the same, it would be some time before we surmised what we thought was the gender of each of the three.

Snowy nest

Across the river from the nest was a large sand pile with an American flag flying atop it. It had been placed there after the attacks on the Twin Towers on 9/11. Of course, we had to try for a shot of that beautiful American symbol together with America's bird.
We salute you both!

The two eaglets hatched sometime around the end of January this first season. By March 18 they were getting to be fairly large.

The eaglets were deep down in the nest as the adult takes off. When an eagle was landing or leaving the nest, any others in the nest would often position themselves to avoid being hit by flapping wings or hanging talons.

On March 20 we captured this shot. It was difficult not to try and imagine what is being communicated by the young eaglet, i.e. "Where is the food?"

Almost two months old now, the eaglets' days were filled with pre-flight learning activities. It began with wing flapping, then flapping and jumping, then jumping and maintaining that height for short periods of time, but with the safety net of the nest right below. These short practice flights also included flying from one side of the nest to the other. This eaglet seemed to be surveying the world outside, living on the edge.

Notice how closely the young eaglets watch the adult as it leaves the nest.

However, at this stage, just over two months old, there was nothing to do but practice, practice, practice!

When the adult left the nest, they observed the wings straight up and its push off for flight. It seemed a perfect example of nature's way of teaching.

Here, an eaglet, about 10 weeks old, went right after the fish the male adult brought to the nest. At this stage the eaglets were getting close to being the same size as the male adult. The male adult is smaller than the female.

There are sometimes some strong breezes in the month of April in this area of Texas. On April 12 the young eaglet was doing his usual pre-flight wing flapping and jumping when a gust of wind suddenly caught it and blew it up and away from the nest, its safety net. As it began frantically flapping, all the onlookers held their breath. Whew! Fortunately, it made it back to the nest okay. It immediately went down deep inside. We did not see the eaglet again for thirty minutes or so. We would have been scared too!

On April 15, at just over 11 weeks of age, one eaglet really flew from the nest, not accidentally this time. A day or so later the other eaglet also fledged. It seemed strange to see the eaglets coming and going as they pleased after their confinement to the nest for all those weeks.

April 30 was one of the last times that season we saw both eaglets with two of the adults as they sat atop one of their favorite perches in the late afternoon sun.

15

By the end of May we were no longer seeing the eagles. They had migrated somewhere. They were not banded, nor tracked and so there was no way to know where they went. It was just a matter of waiting for the fall and their return for the next nesting season.

SECOND NESTING SEASON

The second nesting season we began watching the eagles immediately upon their return from their summer absence. We got our first picture on October 4. We only saw two of the three adults during those first days. (left)

No comment is needed. Everyone who saw the picture below seemed to have his/her own subtitle.

Notice how the nest had deteriorated somewhat while they were away. The white objects in the front of the nest shown here are old turtle shells bleached by the sun.

The first part of November the eagles began working in earnest rebuilding on top of the old nest. They would fly into a limb, grabbing it with their talons, and the force of the impact would snap the limb as can be seen in the photo to the left. Two of them would often work together deciding exactly where and how to fit the limbs together in such a way that they would stay tight and strong through the coming winter.

Work on the nest lasted several weeks, and as you can see, it was beginning to build up.

We often saw the eagles mating. Not only did it take place before the eggs were laid, but also throughout their stay at the nest. It was through this that we surmised the third adult was also a female.

The third adult eagle had been staying a little distance away from the nesting tree and had not been participating in the rebuilding process. Then, on December 11, it landed in the tree on a limb immediately behind the nest. The two other adults, on the right side of the picture, mated twice that morning within a short period of time.

8:47 a.m.	9:15 a.m.

By December 13 they were sitting on eggs, each of the three taking a turn. We could not, of course, see the eggs, nor know how many there were. However, the fact that an adult was constantly nestled down in the bowl of the nest, staying there for long periods of time, seemed a sure indication that the incubation process had begun.

On January 19 there was a definite change in behavior. The adult eagles were constantly coming and going to and from the nest. They also brought food to the nest. We were pretty sure something had hatched, but it was a few days later before the eaglets were large enough to be seen.

We got our first sight of a tiny head on January 29, but it was not until February 5 that we were really able to tell that there were definitely two eaglets in the nest this season.

They grew so fast that it was hard to believe how much they could change from day to day. Look at the difference in the size of the eaglet here on February 14 as compared to the photo above from February 5.

That's right! The eaglets are potty-trained at a very early stage. Actually, we could see them shoot the waste outside the nest before we could see them.

The eaglets could eat too! That's a rather large fish the adult was bringing to the nest on February 15.

February 17 one adult flew across the highway and landed in a pasture nearby. Is there not something a little strange about seeing an adult bald eagle on the ground by a cactus plant?

As they began to lose their grayish down, darker feathers began to grow. At this stage of development, the eaglets were anything but pretty! They were now 5 weeks old.

This shot from March 7 shows how the feathers were getting darker and darker, but there were still gaps in the overall coverage. They were now almost 7 weeks old.

By March 22 the wings were well developed. The eaglets were just two months old.

The adult eagle has a wing span of 6 to 7 feet.

Siblings will be siblings, whether showing off or playing tug-of-war with a turtle.

April 7

On April 8 it was obvious that the eaglets were ready to leave the confines of the nest. The focus of their attention seemed to be more and more on things outside the nest.

April 9 was the big day for the first eaglet to test its wings as it flew outside the immediate nest area. The first landing was very close to the nest - but not in it!

After coming back to the nest, the eaglet was ready to take an intercontinental (okay, intertree) flight. Beginning on the facing page, and continuing on this page is a composite of some of the shots extracted from the photos of that first long flight.

One proud eaglet!

Then, the funniest thing happened. It looked back and saw an adult coming to the nest with a turtle.

The adult was back at the nest...

and the eaglet way over here.

There was only one thing to do...fly back to the nest!

(Above) The eaglet did not stay long in the nest after getting some of the turtle. Its sibling, at this point could only watch. It took its flight two days later. (Left)

(Left) What a sight! Since December 13 we had not seen the nest empty. This must be what they call "empty nest syndrome".   (Right) Just look at the eaglets now on April 16, proud and pretty!

None of the eagles were hanging around the nest very much in May, but we would occasionally see them briefly land in the old tree in front of the nest or fly by the area. Dale Schmidt, Wildlife Technician from Texas Parks and Wildlife, related a story about a friend of his hunting turkey on the Llano River. The hunter had put out his turkey hen decoy and saw some turkey coming in, then they suddenly scattered. One of the eaglets swooped down and attacked the decoy. It tore it apart, apparently trying to get at the meat it thought was there.   After about ten minutes it gave up and flew off.

This second season was basically over for us even though we saw an adult as late as May 18. Again, our question was, would they come again in the fall and use this nest again?

Sunset

Sunrise

THIRD NESTING SEASON

The adult bald eagles were spotted near the nest area in mid-September of the third season but did not seem to hang around the nest much at first. We got our first good picture on October 19.

By the fourth of November they were rebuilding the old nest from last season.

They would work on the building project in the early morning hours and by 9:00 a.m. or so they would be off somewhere else. It took a lot of limbs to get the nest built high and deep enough to protect first the egg(s), and later the eaglet(s).

As the two adults worked together trying to place the limbs in just the right place, there would often be some interesting interactions between them.

(Left and right) The limbs they brought to the nest were not always straight nor easily fitted in just the right place.

(Below) Dale (Texas Parks and Wildlife Technician) tells us in his Forward that an adult will "have a wing span of 6 to 7 feet". Based on the span of the wings below, just how wide was the nest?

The third eagle participated in the rebuilding of the nest this season more than the last one. Her talons and her beak were slightly lighter in color than the other two birds and her feathers were not quite as dark.

On December 5 the behavior of the adults indicated they were already sitting on egg(s). This was earlier than the previous season. Again, each of the three adults would take turns sitting on the egg(s). They would switch every two to four hours.

On January 10 there was a change in the behavior of the adults. They began to look down into the nest as well as bring food to leave for feeding the young.

January 12 brought a strange sight to the nest area. A fourth bald eagle (above right) flew in and landed nearby, but its presence was anything but welcomed by the female on the nest. It called and soon the other female joined it on the nest (above left) and they both called out frantically warning the intruder off. Based on the coloration of the feathers, it was probably a three year old immature eagle. One of the females chased it away but it kept coming back to a nearby tree until the male eagle appeared and joined her in chasing it out of the area.

The adults were very protective of the young. They would not let any other larger birds, whether hawk, osprey, raven, buzzard, gull nor other eagle, stay in the area. The same watchfulness applied to animals that came too close. The tree where the nest is located is a pecan and on several occasions we had seen a squirrel go up into the nest on the bottom side. The adult on the nest would become agitated and keep looking for the source of noise down in the nest. On January 26, the squirrel (highlighted in the photo to the left) came way up on the side of the nest, but his stay was really short-lived as the adult jumped up on the edge of the nest and the squirrel was out of there!

16 days old

20 days old

On January 26 we could clearly see one eaglet.

We were still seeing only one eaglet on January 30.

(Left). By February 2 we were convinced that this year there was just one eaglet. It was growing fast even though the adults did not seem to bring as much food to the nest as in the prior two seasons. There was one less mouth to feed.

(Right) February 9 shows the not so pretty stage of the eaglet's development, when there was a mixture of down and feathers. It was four weeks and two days old.

(Left). By the 13th of February there were some noticeable pin feathers on its growing wings.

It is always nice to have an adult nearby when you are young and growing.

At five weeks of age, the growing feathers were really beginning to show.

A rare sight - all three adults in the nest at one time with the young eaglet. This picture illustrates that not all days are nice and sunny with good photographic lighting. We could not resist adding some pictures taken on cloudy days, such as this shot of the whole family.

Just over 6 weeks old, the eaglet began the all important task of getting its wings ready for the eventual flight that was still 5 or so weeks away.

(Above and right) Eaglet at 7 weeks of age.

The eaglet seemed happy with this catch.

There was an intruder at the nest this day, but from our vantage point we could never see what it was. The female just did not seem too happy with its presence.

When the male brought a fish to the nest (left), the eaglet, in an attempt to get at the fish, grabbed the talon of the adult and then did not seem to want to let it go.

It finally did get its part of the fish.

At just over 8 weeks old, the eaglet begins some serious pre-flight practice with jumping and wing flapping.

The adult watches the practice from below (left) and above (right).

Over the course of the three nesting seasons several limbs in the cottonwood tree, just in front of the nesting tree, broke off during storms and high winds. Several of those limbs had been the favorite perches of the adults when not in the nest. Therefore, they seemed to spend less and less time in the immediate nest area this season. However, occasionally they did land in that tree giving us a chance for some good photo opportunities.

The adults would sometimes take turtle shells out of the nest. Turtles seemed to be their most popular food after fish. They brought in a few birds, a rodent or two and once we saw them bring a jackrabbit. Fish seemed to be the easiest of all the foods to eat. Birds they had to pluck first. They really had to pull at a turtle to get to its meat.

(Below) The adults would wipe their beaks on a limb to clean them after eating.

The young eaglet would quickly grab at anything the adults brought into the nest, hoping for food. Here it only came up with nut grass.

Speaking of food, we want to share with you an illustration showing a peculiar behavior of the third adult. During the second and third nesting seasons one of the nesting pair would bring food to the nest. This third eagle would fly off her perch nearby and gather some grass or a stick and bring it back to the nest. Sometimes, she would antici- pate their arrival and go to the nest with her contri- bution before they brought the food. Any way she did it, she was ready to take control when the food arrived.

Here the third eagle has fluffed her feathers and is making a kind of "fussing sound" to let the other adult know she wanted it out of the nest. (The female was sometimes slower at leaving than the male who appeared to take only so much "fussing".) During this discussion, the fish was left alone and the eaglet cowered in the background waiting for it all to end (left) or trying to figure out what all the racket was about (above).

She usually won these confrontations. Here the other eagle left within a short period of time.

So, we have a confession to make. Since all this third female seemed to do was "keep house" and bring in sticks and grass, we started calling her Heloise after the "Hints from Heloise" columns in the newspaper where Heloise always gave tips about housekeeping. When this particular episode was over, she did not feed the eaglet but rather let it feed itself. It was at that stage of development where it could tear off food anyway.

The fact that the eaglet was beginning to eat on its own reminds us of something that happened the first season. One of the adults brought a turtle to the nest. Wanting to let the eaglets feed themselves, it just put it in the nest and let it lay. The eaglets had evidently not learned that it is better to turn a turtle on its back. This turtle was still alive and it took off across the nest and fell off the side. One eaglet walked over to the side and looked down where it had fallen. It walked back and vocalized to the adult. Again, it walked over to the edge and looked down. Back it went to the adult and vocalized something again. Finally, the adult began looking in the nest and after not seeing anything, began scratching at the grass in the bottom trying to find the turtle!

On a rainy cloudy March 29, it was obvious the eaglet was wanting to fly.

7:08 a.m.

Finally, on March 30, at 11 weeks 2 days old, it fledged. That first flight lasted for over three minutes. It flew to the west...

7:09 a.m.

...it flew to the east....

7:11 a.m.

...it flew all over before finally coming in to land.

A young eaglet when it first flies weighs around 10 pounds. It was sitting on this perch after that long first flight, figiting around a little when suddenly part of the limb where it was sitting broke off!

You can see where the broken limb has fallen. The eaglet managed to keep its composure and inch its way back to the solid part of the limb.

Then, the most interesting thing happened, an almost repeat scene from the year before. An adult brought a turtle to the nest. The eaglet appeared very interested in that turtle, but it took an hour and a half for it to make its way back to the nest.

1. Just a little hop, flight to here...

3...looking up at the nest...

2...then another little hop, flight to here...

4... and slowly made its way back...

8:39 a.m.

5...for that turtle! Okay, so it played with it for a little while before it ate much of it. An eaglet has to learn to fly and carry food at the same time.

67

The eagles brought turtles and American coots to the nest on several occasions. However, when we saw an adult bring this duck into the nest at 9:15 a.m. we knew the coloration was different than anything we had seen before.

April 10. The eaglet came back to the nest and found an empty turtle shell.

April 7. The eaglet had been flying for a week.

This concludes our eagle nest watching for these three years. It has been work, but at the same time, a lot of fun. We end our tale with one of our favorite pictures and add a word of thanks to the eagles who gave us so many opportunities for photographs.

Other photos of foods brought to the nest.

Rodent

Jackrabbit

American Coot

The cottonwood tree in front of the pecan tree where the nest is located had several tall limbs that were broken off during various storms.

The photo below, taken from a different angle, shows the difference with the limbs gone. It also shows the distance between the two trees.

APPENDIX III

DEVELOPMENTAL STAGES OF THE EAGLETS

Two weeks
(left)

Three weeks
(right)

Four weeks
(left)

Five Weeks
(right)

Six weeks (below)

Seven weeks
(left)

Eight weeks
one day
(right)

Nine weeks
(left)

Ten weeks
(right)

11 weeks (below)

APPENDIX V
Etc.
While watching the eagles, there were sometimes periods of inactivity.
Looking around, we saw some of the following things on the roadside.

Blue Curls

(Above) Dew drops on a spider web.   (Below) Sunset on cactus plant.

(Above) Orchard Oriole   (Below) Black Swallowtail on Texas Paintbrush

Cedar Waxwing

Northern Mockingbird

Northern Cardinal

Interesting photographic note:
This photo was taken in the very early morning light, just before sunrise. It was taken at 1/1.6 seconds, F5.6, ISO 200, with a focal length of 850mm. 0 EV. No enhancements have been made to the photo other than a small amount of sharpening and a 50% crop.

INDEX